ZAP!

NIKOLA TESLA
TAKES CHARGE

Monica Kulling   *Illustrated by Bill Slavin*

TUNDRA BOOKS

For Janice and Jon, who visited Tesla's childhood home in Smiljan, Croatia
and found the experience electrifying
M.K.

To my father, who tried to spark my interest in electicity but, sadly,
had a son who couldn't hold a charge
B.S.

Thank you, Sue Tate, for your keen editorial eye and your enthusiasm for the Great Idea series. In particular, thank you for setting me on the right track with this one. Thanks also to electrical engineer Paul Kemp, who reviewed the manuscript, and to Nancy Ennis, my stalwart first reader.

Text copyright © 2016 by Monica Kulling
Illustrations copyright © 2016 by Bill Slavin

Tundra Books, a division of Random House of Canada Limited, a Penguin Random House Company

All rights reserved. The use of any part of this publication reproduced, transmitted in any form or by any means, electronic, mechanical, photocopying, recording, or otherwise, or stored in a retrieval system, without the prior written consent of the publisher – or, in case of photocopying or other reprographic copying, a licence from the Canadian Copyright Licensing Agency – is an infringement of the copyright law.

Library and Archives Canada Cataloguing in Publication

Kulling, Monica, 1952–, author
    Zap! : Nikola Tesla takes charge / Monica Kulling ; illustrated by Bill Slavin.

(Great idea series)
Includes bibliographical references.
Issued in print and electronic formats.
ISBN 978-1-77049-522-7 (bound).–ISBN 978-1-77049-523-4 (epub)

    1. Tesla, Nikola, 1856-1943–Juvenile literature. 2. Electrical engineers–United States–Biography–Juvenile literature. 3. Inventors–United States–Biography–Juvenile literature. 4. Electrification–History–Juvenile literature. 5. Edison, Thomas A. (Thomas Alva), 1847-1931–Juvenile literature. I. Slavin, Bill, illustrator II. Title. III. Title: Nikola Tesla takes charge. IV. Series: Great idea series

TK140.T4K85 2016   j621.3092   C2015-903856-1
                                             C2015-903857-X

Published simultaneously in the United States of America by Tundra Books of Northern New York, a division of Random House of Canada Limited, a Penguin Random House Company

Library of Congress Control Number: 2015941403

Sources of Inspiration:

Carlson, W. Bernard. *Tesla: Inventor of the Electrical Age*. New Jersey: Princeton University Press, 2013.

Cheney, Margaret. *Tesla: Man Out of Time*. New York: Touchstone Books, 2001.

Rusch, Elizabeth. *Electrical Wizard: How Nikola Tesla Lit Up the World*. Massachusetts: Candlewick Press, 2013.

Seifer, Marc. *Wizard: The Life and Times of Nikola Tesla: Biography of a Genius*, reprint edition. New York: Citadel Press – Kensington, 2011.

Tesla, Nikola. *My Inventions and Other Writings*. New York: Penguin Classics, 2011.

Internet:

http://www.fi.edu/learn/case-files/tesla/index.html

http://www.physics4kids.com/files/elec_ac.html

Edited by Sue Tate
Designed by Leah Springate
The artwork in this book was created with pen and ink on paper and digitally colored.
The text was set in Minion
Printed and bound in China

www.penguinrandomhouse.ca

1   2   3   4   5   20   19   18   17   16

Electric Cat

Niko, at three, loves Macak.
He strokes the cat's silky back.

The winter air is cold and dry.
Niko's touch makes the sparks fly.

"It's electricity," says Papa.

But why?

"It's electrons and protons.
Negative and positive,"
Papa explains.

"It's magic! It's mystery!"
Niko exclaims.

An ocean liner steamed into New York Harbor. It was 1884. A young man named Nikola Tesla walked down the gangplank. He was excited and a little nervous. America was different from the European cities he'd lived in. Would he be happy here?

On the ship, Tesla had been robbed. He was left with four cents in his pocket, a book of poems, a drawing of a flying machine, and a letter of introduction to Thomas Edison, the "electrical wizard" of America.

Nikola Tesla was born in 1856 in Smiljan, Croatia. A summer storm had raged that night. Lightning flashed – *zap!* – and Tesla was born as July 9th became July 10th. The family called him Niko.

Niko's memory was astonishing. He knew six languages by age ten.

When he saw an engraving of Niagara Falls, Niko exclaimed, "One day I will go to America and put a giant waterwheel under the falls!"

What an extraordinary thing to say! thought his family. But that was Niko's way.

Now Nikola Tesla was walking the streets of Lower Manhattan. He was searching for an address he'd memorized. Up ahead, he saw a man working on a broken machine.

Tesla knew engines. "Would you like my help?" he asked.

"Why not?" the discouraged man replied.

Tesla fixed the machine, and the man gave him twenty dollars.

Life in America was off to a good start!

Tesla was looking for Thomas Edison's factory. He knew that the inventor had so many ideas that he hired young men to help develop them. Might he give Tesla a job?

The Edison Machine Works was crowded and noisy. Men worked at benches while all around them wheels whirred and pulleys screeched.

Thomas Edison was on the telephone in his office. Nikola Tesla waited patiently.

"I know just the person for the job!" bellowed Edison into the mouthpiece. "I'll send him right over!"

An ocean liner called the SS *Oregon* couldn't sail. Its dynamo wasn't working. The ship's dynamo powered lights and was vital. No one in the workshop knew enough about electricity to fix it. And Edison was too busy.

Edison hung up the phone, mumbling, "I don't know a soul who can do that job."

Nikola Tesla stepped forward and cleared his throat.

"Can I help you, mister?" asked Edison, rumpled and frustrated.

Tesla gave Edison the letter from his boss in Paris. It began, "My dear Edison, I know two great men and you are one of them. The other is this young man!"

Edison sent Tesla to fix the SS *Oregon*'s dynamo. The young man worked all day and through the night.

In the early morning, Tesla was walking back to his hotel when Edison came upon him.

"So you've been out all night having fun, have you?" barked Edison.

"I've finished the job," replied Tesla. "The ship has already sailed."

Edison was astounded. Tesla had finished the work faster than he'd thought possible. He offered Tesla a job on the spot.

Nikola Tesla came to America with a dream. In 1882, he'd had a vision of a motor that ran on alternating current electricity. But he had no money to build it.

In *direct* current, the electrical current always flows in the same direction between the positive and negative terminals. In *alternating* current, the direction reverses, or alternates, sixty times per second.

But Thomas Edison was only interested in his own system. "The future belongs to direct current," he said.

"Machines would be more efficient if they ran on alternating current," explained Tesla. "Parts would not break down so often. You could send power over great distances and not have to build as many power stations."

But Edison had invested a lot of time and money in his system. He didn't want to give it up. He offered Tesla fifty thousand dollars to make direct current more efficient.

When the work was done, Edison refused to pay.

Tesla quit. Digging ditches was the only work he could find. "It was the lowest point of my life," Tesla later wrote.

Things looked bleak. Then Tesla met George Westinghouse, who thought that alternating current was the way to electrify America.

Westinghouse paid for the right to use Tesla's ideas in his own work. He also gave Tesla a job.

Tesla moved to Pittsburgh, Pennsylvania, where he lived in the Hotel Anderson. He would always live in hotels.

By 1887, Thomas Edison had built 121 power stations. Direct current was weaker than alternating current. A house more than a mile from a power station didn't get full power. More and more power stations had to be built. Direct current motors were also costly to maintain.

But people trusted Thomas Edison, so they believed that direct current was better. Besides, Edison had lit the millionaire J.P. Morgan's mansion. Nikola Tesla was a man few people knew or understood.

Edison wanted to make Tesla's system look harmful. He put ads in papers warning people that alternating current could kill them. He publicly electrocuted dogs, cats, and even an elephant using Tesla's system.

Soon people were afraid. So Tesla began a campaign of his own. In 1891, he invented the Tesla Coil. With this device, he safely passed nearly one million volts of electricity across his body.

Tesla held a lightbulb in one hand and touched the coil. The bulb glowed. These displays helped the public see that electricity could be safe. Still, the question remained: who would light America?

In 1893, the World's Fair came to Chicago. Everyone wondered which system would light the grand buildings and wide walkways.

Edison said he could do the job for $1.8 million. Westinghouse bid $399,000. He won the contract.

The fair ran for six months. During that time, 27 million people saw a light display like no other before it. America was electrified!

In 1895, Tesla and Westinghouse built a generator at Niagara Falls. As the date for throwing the switch drew near, people grew more and more excited.

At midnight, November 16, 1896, the switch was thrown. The hydroelectric power plant sent power as far as Buffalo, New York: 20 miles (32 kilometers) away.

Tesla's childhood dream had come true. He'd harnessed the power of one of nature's most popular wonders, Niagara Falls.

Tesla's Robot

Tesla had a new marvel. It was a radio-controlled boat. He brought it to the Electrical Exhibition in New York City in 1898. A crowd stood around a tank of water to watch the inventor move the boat across the water without touching it.

Tesla worked controls on a device that sent out radio waves to an antenna on the boat. In 1898, no one knew what radio waves were or how they might be used from a distance. It was Marconi who sent the first radio signal across the Atlantic in 1901, but he used ideas that Tesla had patented years before.

The boat in the pool of water moved across the tank and back again, as Tesla worked the controls. It was magic! The boat seemed to sail by itself.

Tesla told the crowd, "One day, we will make robots that do our work."

As usual, Tesla's predictions were years ahead of their time!